D1409751

The Complete Guides to Horses and Ponies

HORSE&PONY BREEDS

Jackie Budd

Gareth Stevens Publishing
MILWAUKEE

For a free color catalog describing Gareth Stevens
Publishing's list of high-quality books and
multimedia programs, call 1-800-542-2595 (USA)
or 1-800-461-9120 (Canada).
Gareth Stevens Publishing's Fax: 414) 225-0377.
See our catalog, too, on the World Wide Web:
http://gsinc.com

Library of Congress Cataloging-in-Publication Data

Budd, Jackie.
Horse and pony breeds/by Jackie Budd.
p. cm.—(The complete guides to horses and ponies)
"First published in 1996 by Ringpress Books . . .
England"—T.p. verso.
Includes index.
Summary: Highlights beautiful and unusual
breeds of horses and ponies, from tough native
ponies around the world to the heavy horses
that pull their own weight for a living.
ISBN 0-8368-2046-0 (lib. bdg.)
1. Horse breeds—Juvenile literature.
2. Horses—Juvenile literature. 3. Ponies—Juvenile
literature. [1. Horse breeds. 2. Horses. 3. Ponies.]
I. Title. II. Series:
Budd, Jackie. Complete guides to horses and ponies.
SF291.B78 1998
636.1—dc21 97-31767

First published in North America in 1998
by **Gareth Stevens Publishing**
1555 North RiverCenter Drive, Suite 201
Milwaukee, WI 53212 USA

This U.S. edition © 1998 by Gareth Stevens, Inc.
Created with original © 1996 Ringpress Books Ltd.
and Jackie Budd, P. O. Box 8, Lydney, Gloucestershire,
United Kingdom, GL15 6YD, in association with
Horse & Pony Magazine. All photographs courtesy
of Horse & Pony Magazine, except page 40 (Barb)
by Bob Langrish. The photos of the Hanoverian
(Donna Sommer and Annual Revue, page 46) are
reproduced by kind permission of Mr. A. Ackerhurst
of the British Hanoverian Horse Society, the Holstein
(Maximillian Salut) by kind permission of the
Maximillian Stud, the Irish Draft (Roma Atlantic
Moonshine) by kind permission of Mrs. A. Addams-
Williams, and page 56 (Quarter Horse) by Glyn Mead.
Additional end matter © 1998 Gareth Stevens, Inc.

The publisher would like to thank Kate Considine,
an experienced rider and trainer, for her assistance
with the accuracy of the text. Ms. Considine
showed in Switzerland for 2-1/2 years and has
worked with Olympians from the USA.
Currently, she is showing and training hunters
and jumpers in the United States.

Printed in Mexico

1 2 3 4 5 6 7 8 9 02 01 00 99 98

CONTENTS

Little and large — the world's largest horse, Boringdon Black King, poses with a Shetland pal.

What is a breed?

The long and the short of it . . .

THERE are more than two hundred official breeds of horses and ponies in the world today. Breeds are groups of horses that always reproduce particular features, such as height, stride, shape (called conformation), and sometimes color, that make them different from other types.

Some breeds are extremely old and have been created in a natural way. Perhaps a herd of ponies has been isolated in a certain region and, as they have bred among themselves, all look the same.

Today, however, many breeds come into existence through selective breeding to produce a certain type of horse or pony, usually with a particular job or work in mind. In this instance, breeders choose only the best mares and stallions that show the typical features of the breed.

Many breeds today are not pure but are the result of mixing or crossing different breeds to get the best combination of good or useful features.

To be called a breed, a group has to always breed true to type. This means its characteristics must always be passed on to its foals.

These features are clearly defined, often by a breed society that keeps a special list, called a stud book. This book details the individual horses belonging to that breed, along with their pedigrees.

A Lipizzaner shows its powerful movement.

Welsh Cobs are strong and full of energy and presence.

Centuries ago, the Spanish rode to war on the proud and fiery Andalusian. Today, these horses are known for high stepping.

Horses have been popular throughout history for their colorful markings.

DID YOU KNOW?

ALTHOUGH they are different species, asses and horses can be bred together. A mule is the offspring of a female horse and a male ass. A hinny is the offspring of a female ass and a male horse. But these strong, tough equines rarely produce their own young because they are usually infertile.

How did breeds develop?

THE horse belongs to a genus (or animal group) called *Equus*. It is easy to spot the members of the horse family because they all have a single-toed hoof on the end of each leg. So, among the horse's relatives alive today, we can recognize zebras, donkeys, asses, and mules. Yet, despite being so different in appearance, Shetlands, Shires, Arabians, and asses all share common ancestors.

The First Horses

THE very first horses were tiny, scampering, deer-like creatures that lived in a tropical habitat 65 million years ago. They were called *Hyracotherium*. They browsed on leaves and had padded feet with four toes to keep them from sinking in the marshy ground.

Over millions of years, changes in the climate and environment meant animals with certain features survived better than others. Many species disappeared, and others changed in appearance.

The horse's ancestors were great survivors. As their surroundings slowly altered from lush forests to dry, open grasslands, they grew taller and adapted to eating grass. With very sharp senses and long legs — that gradually lost some toes — they became well equipped to escape predators and stay alive. By the end of the last Ice Age (15,000 years ago), the many different types of horses were down to just a single genus, *Equus*, with its one-toed hoof, perfect for galloping.

Millions of these horses roamed over land bridges from their homeland in America to Asia and Europe.

The Horse Family

DIFFERENT types of *Equus* developed in different parts of the world. Animals that migrated early and moved south to the hot regions of Africa, the Middle East, and southern Asia became the wild asses and zebras. The donkey is descended from the African ass.

A closer relative to the domesticated horse is the Asiatic Wild Horse, called Przewalski's Horse, after the explorer who discovered a herd of them in Mongolia in 1881.

Przewalski's Horse has changed little since prehistoric times.

This is a distinct species that is ancient and looks much like the horses shown in prehistoric cave paintings. Now, only a few remain in zoos, but breeders are trying to reintroduce them in the wild.

The most numerous type that developed from the migrating primitive herds was called *Equus caballus*. This species sorted itself into two broad groups. In hot, dry southern regions, lightly built, fast-moving, sensitive horses developed. These were called hot-bloods because of their fiery temperaments. The Arabian is descended from this type. Hot bloods adapted to the scorching environment with fine skin, lean legs, a high-set tail, and a small, tapering head with large nostrils to filter out dusty air.

Farther north, vegetation was lush and the ground was damp. Big, heavy, slow-moving horses developed there that became known as cold-bloods. Smaller types also spread across Europe and Asia, learning to survive in remote areas in bleak conditions. These developed into the native pony breeds that stayed tiny. They grew incredibly thick coats and long manes and tails for protection against bitter weather.

The domestic donkey (left). *A mule* (right) *is a cross between two species — a horse and an ass.*

Domesticating the Horse

THE hot-bloods and the cold-bloods existed by the time humans began domesticating the horse, about five thousand years ago. Then, as people found more and more uses for them, horses became highly valued helpers in the development of civilization.

Horses have played a central role in history ever since. Their speed and muscle power have been utilized in agriculture, transportation, industry, and war. In modern times, machines have taken over traditional jobs, but, increasingly, horses are finding a role in sport and pleasure riding.

Breeds Are Born

OF course, it wasn't long before even the earliest humans found that, by breeding certain horses with others, they could produce a foal that was especially strong, fast, and easy to handle.

Regional breeds began to develop that were particularly well suited to the area and the type of work required.

As civilizations spread and traded with each other, horses that had developed in certain areas of the world could be bred with those from other areas.

Since that time, humans have been influential in the way the horse looks — mixing types to create the many shapes and sizes of horses we know today, then classifying them according to different breeds.

Cold-bloods, like the Shire, became tall, heavy, and slow-moving.

A full, wavy mane and tail are typical of the Dartmoor pony. The Fjord's (inset) distinctive coloring shows ancient ancestry.

Pony

Officially, a pony is a horse that measures 14.2 hands high or less. One hand equals 4 inches (10.2 centimeters). But ponies are not just little horses. Only a few breeds, like the Caspian and Falabella, are true miniature horses that have horse features, but on a small scale. In general, many features other than size set ponies apart from their larger relatives.

Most ponies are incredibly strong for their size; they are tough and hardy. They have short legs in relation to their bodies and usually move with short, quick strides. When first born, a pony foal is generally a mini-version of the adult, already in proportion, compared to a horse foal that usually has long, gangly legs. Ponies are famous for their quick thinking and their native cunning, which have helped them survive in the harshest conditions.

Many pony breeds are ancient — they are closer to the original ancestors of the horse. In fact, most horse breeds developed from ponies. The variety of pony breeds shows how important they have been to farms, as pack animals, and for pulling carts. Ponies are still at work in some countries, but most are bred for children to enjoy.

All of the Welsh ponies originated from the tough, little Welsh Mountain.

Breeds

Arabian blood helped make the Connemara (right) one of the prettiest native ponies.

Highland

Place of origin: Scotland

Height: 13-14.2hh

Color: Dun, gray, black, or brown are most common. Bay or chestnut with a silvery mane and tail can also be found. There should be no, or few, white markings. Most ponies have a dorsal stripe along the back. Many also have zebra-marks inside the forelegs — signs of their primitive origins.

Character: Hardy, powerful but dependable.

Conformation: The Highland has a broad, short head with small ears and a large jaw. The neck is strong and arched. The body is deep and compact with a short back and powerful quarters, making the pony extremely strong. The short, sturdy legs are lightly feathered and help it make its way surefootedly over mountain terrain.

DID YOU KNOW?

THE Highland is the largest of Britain's nine native breeds of ponies.

THINK of a traditional Scottish sight, and you might picture a Highland pony. It is laden with a deer-hunter's gear, harnessed to a wagon, or in a line of holiday-makers riding across a heather-covered moor.

Highland ponies are part of Scotland's history. For hundreds of years, these stocky animals were the main form of transportation in this mountainous country. From pulling peat-carts and hauling logs, to carrying game or herding sheep, this versatile and surefooted pony worked hard for the Scottish people, who have always loved and valued it.

Today, machines have taken over many of the historical jobs, but Highlands are popular riding and driving ponies. They make safe and sturdy mounts for trail rides. Breeders use the Highland's qualities of hardiness and strength to cross with other, finer breeds to produce hunters and competition horses.

Although there were ponies in the north of Scotland in the Ice Age, the origins of the Highland pony have been lost over time. Unlike the Exmoor, the Highland was never cut off from outside influences, and, today, some traces of Arabian blood can be seen in many Highlands.

Early records tell of a typical Highland being ridden by King Robert the Bruce in the fourteenth century. By the 1700s, droves of ponies were being herded south to be sold across the border. The poet Robert Burns mentioned the breed. Later, better roads brought tourists and sports enthusiasts to Scotland to enjoy the scenery from pony-back. Queen Victoria started keeping Highlands at Balmoral. Studs were set up, both by private landowners and the government, to breed the very best ponies.

Exmoor

THE Exmoor is Britain's most ancient breed of pony, and it is special in many ways. Its ancestors roamed the West Country moors as far back as the Bronze Age, one hundred thousand years ago.

Ponies that look very much like the Exmoors of today are portrayed in historical carvings pulling Celtic and Roman chariots. The carvings were discovered in Somerset, the home of the Exmoor. Fossils discovered in Alaska show similarities, leading scientists to think that the Exmoor is among the closest of all breeds to the horse's primitive forebears.

The Exmoor is thought to be the foundation for almost all of Britain's other native ponies. It is still used today to add a touch of hardiness and pony cleverness to larger breeds. The moors where Exmoor ponies lived were so bleak and isolated that the breed not only became tough, it also remained pure. That is why all the ponies look alike. Although ponies still run in herds on the moors, they are all owned and registered. Every year, the ponies are rounded up and inspected. Those that reach the breed standard are branded with a star, an individual number, and a herd number.

For centuries, farmers used the ponies as pack animals and for herding sheep, but now the Exmoor's role is changing. Sadly, the pony is a threatened breed, with just over 770 purebreds left. However, this sturdy and quick-witted breed is starting to make a comeback as a children's riding and driving pony.

FACT FILE

Place of origin: Britain (Devon/Somerset)

Height: Mares up to 12.2hh; stallions up to 12.3hh

Color: Brown, bay, or dun, with distinctive "mealy" areas around the muzzle, eyes, and flanks. No white.

Character: Intelligent, tough, independent.

Conformation: The Exmoor has a short, chunky head with small ears, a wide forehead, and distinctively prominent, hooded, or "toad" eyes. Its large teeth are well suited to biting off and chewing coarse grass. Deep, wide chests provide lots of lung and heart room to help with stamina. The back is level and strong. The legs are short, straight, and sturdy. In winter, the ponies grow a dense, woolly undercoat covered by a rough, longer overcoat that keeps them warm in the worst of conditions. Rainwater drains from the outer coat, keeping the pony dry. A fan of tail hair over the dock helps protect the quarters from the wind.

Connemara

THE Connemara pony has lived in the bleak area of bogs and mountains of Galway, in the west of Ireland, since ancient times.

Over the years, many other breeds have been added to the native stock to refine it into one of the world's most attractive and athletic ponies.

Legend says that horses shipwrecked off the Irish coast from the Spanish Armada gave the Connemaras their touch of class. But this quality is more likely to have been inherited from their forerunner, the Irish Hobby, which was a cross between the local ponies and Barb and Spanish horses, imported in the sixteenth and seventeenth centuries.

Ponies were used for every farm task — from plowing to pulling carts loaded with potatoes, corn, or seaweed from the beaches. Later, when breeders were concerned about a deterioration in quality, some Arabian blood was added along with Welsh Cob, Thoroughbred, Hackney, and Irish Draft. This mix produced a pony with all the common sense and toughness of its wild ancestors, with the bonus of speed and jumping ability. Today's Connemaras, which grow bigger than those that live wild in their native region, can easily carry an adult. They have good conformation and, when crossed with other breeds, such as the Thoroughbred, make great competitors. They have been exported worldwide.

FACT FILE

Place of origin: Ireland
Height: 13-14.2hh
Color: Often gray, also bay, brown, black, or dun. Sometimes chestnut or roan.
Character: Tough, agile, intelligent, brave, hardy, and reliable.
Conformation: The Connemara's neat, attractive head with its straight profile and big, bold eyes show some of its Asian background. For a pony, it has especially good length of rein, and sloping shoulders, which give it a comfortable, flowing, and athletic stride. Its body is compact and deep, and the quarters are rounded and strong. The legs are clean but sturdy, often with 7-8 inches (17-20 cm) of bone.

FACT FILE

Place of origin: England (Devon)

Height: Up to 12.2hh

Color: Mostly brown, black, or bay. Sometimes gray, chestnut, or roan. White markings not encouraged.

Character: Hardy, dependable, agile, sensitive, and kind.

Conformation: The Dartmoor has particularly good conformation for a native pony. It has a small, fine, "pony" head with small, alert ears and bright eyes. The head is well set onto a strong neck that is not too short. The shoulders are very sloping. The body is deep and of medium length, with well-muscled quarters. The Dartmoor always has a full, thick mane and tail and slender but tough little legs. It is famous for its good balance and free, low-striding movement.

DID YOU KNOW?

DURING the 1940s, the breed almost became extinct, with only two stallions and twelve mares registered in the Stud Book. Now it is thriving once again.

DARTMOOR ponies originally lived on the high, windswept moorlands of Devon in southwestern England, where a few ponies still breed in the wild.

Reference is made to the ponies as far back as the year 1012, but little is known about how they came to look as they do today. Perhaps some Asian horses were introduced onto the moors several hundred years ago. In the last century, trotters, Welsh ponies and cobs, Arabians, Exmoors, and small

Thoroughbreds may have been bred with them. There was a plan to use Shetlands to create "pit" ponies for work in the mines, but this turned out to be a disaster.

The result of all this interbreeding is a stocky but pretty pony with a lot more "class" than its ancestors. The Dartmoor was used by local people for hauling loads of metal from the tin mines to town. Now breeding is carefully controlled, and the hardy and trusty Dartmoor is gaining a reputation as a perfect first riding pony.

Fell

THE Fell is a close cousin of the Dales pony and lives on the west side of the Pennines in northern England in the area called the Lake District. Both breeds share much the same roots but developed slightly differently as they were put to different uses.

The early Fells were descendants of local moorland ponies and the black Friesian horses brought by Roman invaders to the northern outposts.

These became crossed with fast, hardy Galloways, ponies used by the Scottish sheep and cattle drovers and border raiders during the Middle Ages. Over the years, the Fell was used as a pack pony, but also for herding over the rocky crags and valleys.

Droves of heavily laden ponies were taken as far as London until the railways took over as a means of transporting goods and raw materials for industry.

With its naturally active trot, the Fell was especially handy in harness and is popular today both as a riding and driving pony.

DID YOU KNOW?

IN the eighteenth century, Fells carried loads of 210 pounds (95 kilograms) up to 240 miles (385 kilometers) a week.

FACT FILE

Place of origin: England (northwest)
Height: 13-14hh
Color: Black, bay, brown, gray.
Character: Alert, strong, courageous, tough, with great stamina.
Conformation: The Fell has a small head with a broad forehead, bright eyes, and wide nostrils. Its shoulders are strong, but sloping. Its body is long and very powerful. The legs are sturdy with a minimum of 8 inches (20 cm) of bone and covered with fine feathering. Both the knees and hocks have a lot of flexion, creating an energetic, straight, ground-covering stride.

THE early Dales ponies were such speedy trotters they could cover a mile (1.6 km) in three minutes, even with a heavy rider on board.

Dales

DALES ponies originate from the upland areas in northeastern England, across the Pennine hills from their close, but smaller, relation, the Fell. Strong and agile, the Dales were used for centuries in the mines. They were also used as pack ponies to carry heavy loads of lead and coal across the moors to the coastal ports.

When railways and trucks took over their jobs, Dales ponies worked on the hill farms and with the army, pulling loads weighing over a ton.

The Dales was only recognized as a separate breed to the Fell at the end of the 1800s. Many ponies can be traced back to a Welsh Cob, named Comet, foaled in 1851.

The pony's stocky build also comes from the crossing with Clydesdale workhorses during this time. The high-stepping trot of the Welsh Cob can be seen in today's Dales, which are ideal for driving in harness. Dales ponies also make great trail ride and family riding ponies. They can carry an adult easily, and they are hardy and kind natured. Although the breed almost died out in the twentieth century, it is now thriving.

Place of origin: Britain (northeast)
Height: Up to 14.2hh
Color: Usually black; sometimes brown, gray, or bay; occasionally roan.
Character: Bold, intelligent, calm, and unflappable; also energetic and determined.
Conformation: The Dales pony has a neat, straight head with bright eyes set well apart and small ears that curve in. The long, muscled neck is well set onto sloping shoulders, helping the pony cover the ground. Being short and compact, the back is strong and the quarters very powerful. The chest is broad and deep, providing the breed's famous stamina. The Dales is renowned for its hard, well-shaped feet and the dense, flat bones of its legs, which are short and covered around the pasterns with silky, straight feathering.

THE Shetland is the smallest of Britain's native ponies, with a history that stretches back to the eighth century.

It is believed that Shetland ponies roamed the hills and moors of the bleak and remote islands to the north of Scotland before the time of the Norse invasions.

The first of these ponies might have come from Scandinavia, across the icefields of ten thousand years ago, or they might be related to dwarf ponies brought by the first Stone Age settlers.

For hundreds of years, Shetland Islanders have grazed these sturdy little ponies on sparse few acres (hectares) of common grazing land called *scattald*. They have produced a breed famous for toughness and hardiness.

Many ponies still live on the windy, heather-covered moors and beaches of their native homeland. Shetlands have been invaluable workers for farmers, carrying burdens of peat fuel for fires and seaweed to fertilize the fields. They have been used for transportation and tilling the land. During the nineteenth century, when children were banned from working in the mines, black Shetland stallions were bred as pit ponies. Today, Shetlands can be found throughout the world. They are ridden, shown, driven, used in the circus, and chosen as a favorite first pony.

Despite a reputation for being rather stubborn at times, a well-trained and firmly handled Shetland makes a great friend that can take part in many activities. It can accomplish much more than its tiny stature suggests.

DID YOU KNOW?

THE Shetland can carry more weight in relation to its size than any other horse or pony breed.

Shetland

FACT FILE

Place of origin: Britain (Shetland and Orkney Islands)

Height: Not over 42 inches (107 cm) at four years or older. Ponies as small as 28 inches (72 cm) are found, but those that are specially bred smaller than this are called miniatures.

Color: Commonly black, but any color except spotted.

Character: Resilient, independent, nimble, willful but kind.

Conformation: The Shetland has a small head with a slightly dished face. It has a broad forehead and a strong jaw for making the most of poor grazing. Its eyes are large, bright, and bold. The nostrils are wide for warming cold air. Its legs are short, solid, and straight, set well apart with tough little feet. This makes it surefooted but able to cover the ground with a flowing stride.

New Forest

THE New Forest, a large area of heath, bogs, and woodland in southern England, was once the hunting ground of kings. Ponies still roam and graze the Forest, which is now one of the widest unenclosed stretches of land in the south.

Herds of ponies lived alongside other wild animals as far back as Roman times. In 1016, these ponies were recorded in King Canute's Forest Law. Perhaps because of the position of the Forest near the busy port of Southampton and trade routes to the West Country, the ponies have been influenced by many other breeds over the centuries. Welsh mares were released there in 1208. In the eighteenth and nineteenth centuries, Thoroughbred, Arabian, and Barb stallions, and many of the other British native breeds lived there. A well-known polo pony also lived in the Forest early in the 1900s. But since 1938, no outside crossbreeding has been allowed. It is surprising that, with this large mixture of ancestors, the New Forest pony still has a distinctive look.

It has certainly kept its docile character, hardiness, strength, and agility, which make it a popular, all-around family pony. It is in demand around the world as a clever performer. Breeders like to cross it with Arabian and Thoroughbred for all kinds of horse sports, especially cross-country. Each autumn, the ponies in the Forest are rounded up. Most of the foals go to an annual sale.

Place of origin: Britain (southwest Hampshire)
Height: Not over 14.2hh, usually over 12hh
Color: Mostly bay and brown, but any color except pinto.
Character: Easy to handle and train, kind, hardy, reliable.
Conformation: The New Forest pony has an intelligent head, well set onto the neck, with long, sloping shoulders. This makes it comfortable for people to ride with a free, low, long-striding movement suited to the Forest environment. The body is deep but narrow in frame, with strong quarters. The legs are sturdy, with hard, round feet. Larger ponies are easily strong enough to carry an adult.

FACT FILE

DID YOU KNOW?

MANY New Forest ponies share an ancestor with Eclipse, one of the greatest racehorses that ever lived.

Welsh

THERE are four distinct kinds of Welsh ponies and cobs. They are registered in their breed society's Stud Book under the sections — A, B, C, and D.

Although they vary quite a lot in size and looks, all derive from the smallest one, the tough and pretty Welsh Mountain pony. It has been bred in the wild hills of Wales since Celtic times.

As far back as the Romans, people improved the hardy local hill ponies by crossing them with Arabians and other Asian breeds that traders brought to Britain. This continued over the years, with several Arabian, Barb, and Thoroughbred horses recorded as being widely used from the eighteenth century onward.

Two ponies in particular, Dyoll Starlight, foaled in 1894, and his great great grandson, Coed Coch Glydwr, are considered to be the founders of the modern, refined Section A Welsh Mountain.

The larger Section B Welsh ponies came from Mountain ponies that grew too large, often crossed with Arabians and small Cobs or Thoroughbreds. They made useful herding ponies and, later, eye-catching rides for showing and competition. By the fifteenth century, the addition of extra Cob blood led to the Section C, Welsh Pony of Cob Type.

This was a slightly chunkier version, ideal as a harness and hunting pony, suited to every job around the hill farm, and put to use as a pack pony for the North Wales slate mines.

Finally, the Section D Welsh Cob was established by adding more Barb, Spanish, Hackney, and light carriage horse to the smaller types. This produced a chunky, medium-sized little horse with all the strength, hardiness, and quick wits of a pony.

Formerly, the Cobs were in demand by the army and for pulling delivery vehicles in the growing cities. Today, they are the world's most famous ride-and-drive breed, with power and presence and a spectacular high-stepping trot. When crossed with the Thoroughbred, in particular, they make fantastic all-around performance horses.

> **Place of origin:** Wales
> **Color:** Any solid color. Gray is most common in Welsh Mountain ponies; many Cobs are black or bay.
> **Character:** Intelligent, spirited, kind, hardy, and brave.

DID YOU KNOW?

WHEN Henry Tudor arrived in Wales in 1485 on his way to victory in the Wars of the Roses, the Welsh army was mounted on Welsh Cobs.

THE Australian Pony is descended from Welsh ponies of the eighteenth and nineteenth centuries.

Section C (Welsh Pony, Cob Type)

Height: Up to 13.2hh
Conformation: Based on the Welsh Mountain, but more Cob, Hackney, and Spanish influence has created a sturdier, stockier version of the Section B. Suited to harness work as well as riding activities, especially jumping and trail rides.

Section A [Welsh Mountain]
Height: Not over 12hh
Conformation: The head should be small and neat, and it sometimes shows a slight Arabian-like dished profile and wide forehead. It has tiny, erect ears and big, dark eyes. The neck is muscular and arched, and the sloping shoulder gives a free-striding movement. The legs are fine but sturdy, with dense, hard little feet. The deep, compact body has lots of heart and lung room for such a small pony. The tail is always set high and carried grandly. Welsh ponies are famed for their active paces with a great amount of

flexion in the knees and the hocks, coming from their powerful hindquarters. This high action helps them cross rough and difficult ground quickly, while keeping their balance.

Section B [Welsh Pony]
Height: Up to 13.2hh
Conformation: Similar to the Welsh Mountain, but with a little more substance and more of the qualities of a riding pony, such as greater slope to the shoulder and length in the neck. It has particularly straight movement, and its stride is longer and lower than the Section A, making it a comfortable ride and a good jumper.

Section D [Welsh Cob]
Height: Over 13.2hh — mainly 14.2hh-15.2hh
Conformation: The Welsh Cob's handsome head shows quality and strength but has a definite pony air about it. The eyes are dark, bold, and intelligent. The forehead is wide, the ears are neat and well set, and the nostrils are large and wide. The Cob's outline is the same as the Mountain pony. The Welsh Cob's striking movement comes from powerful flexion of the hocks behind and in front, and huge extension of the forelegs that are lifted from the shoulder and flung as far forward as possible in all the paces.

FACT FILE

FACT FILE

FACT FILE

Fjord

THE Norwegian Fjord is one of the most distinctive of all pony breeds. It is also one of the oldest. With its pale dun coat, eel stripe along the back, and zebra markings on the legs, the Fjord is very similar in looks to the primitive Przewalski's Horse.

The Vikings rode Fjords into battle, as depicted in many ancient carvings. These hardy ponies traveled with their warlike masters across the seas to Iceland and the islands of Scotland, where they influenced other native breeds. The Vikings were the first people to use horses for plowing.

The Fjord ponies have been used for centuries on the land as sturdy and surefooted pack ponies and all-around trusty workers. Although many still earn their keep in the traditional way on their native Scandinavian mountain farms, the Fjords have also found fame worldwide as first-class riding and driving ponies and highly capable competitors — especially in driving, endurance, and vaulting.

DID YOU KNOW?

FJORD ponies today still have their manes cut in the same way as they did in Viking times. By tradition, the coarse hair is trimmed so it stands up stiffly in a curve. The black hair in the middle can be seen above the silver.

FACT FILE

Place of origin: Norway
Height: 13-14.2hh
Color: Any shade of dun, with a dorsal stripe from tail to forelock. The mane is dark in the center and silver on the outside. The legs are dark and often have zebra marks.
Character: Hardy, strong and brave, gentle, willing; can also be independent.
Conformation: The Fjord has a typical short pony head with a wide forehead, large cheeks, bold eyes, and small, alert ears. It has fairly upright shoulders, a broad chest, and a round body and quarters. Its short, straight legs are built for strength and soundness and have a little feathering around the heels.

Haflinger

HAFLINGER ponies, with their unmistakable golden coloring, can be seen today in their southern Austrian homeland. They work on the steep Alpine slopes, pulling sleighs and carts, as they have done for centuries.

The pony has a long history in this region. It was established by crossing native Tyrolean mountain ponies with Arabian horses brought back from wars with the Turks. In fact, all purebred Haflingers trace back to one particular Arabian stallion called El Bedavi XXII. He gave his offspring eastern spirit and elegance to add to their native soundness and agility. It was his son, Folie 29, that first showed the chestnut coat and white mane and tail that is now the hallmark of all Haflingers. Because it has been isolated in the mountains for so many years, the Haflinger breed has remained very pure. All the ponies look similar.

Growing up on the Alpine slopes has made these ponies very tough. By breathing the thin air, the youngsters develop strong hearts and lungs. Many are very long-lived, often reaching forty years of age or more.

During the coldest and wettest part of winter, the ponies are traditionally brought into stables that are built underneath the farmhouses. So, although they are easy-keepers, they are not as hardy as many other native breeds.

The Haflinger has a close cousin in the Italian Avelignese pony, which is often bigger but shares the same ancestry. Nowadays, Haflingers can be found all around the world. They are active and trustworthy; popular as family ponies for all-around riding and in harness.

FACT FILE

Place of origin: Austria (southern Tyrol)
Height: Mares 13.1-14.2hh; stallions/geldings 13.3-14.25hh
Color: Chestnut, varying from light to liver or deep red, with a flaxen mane and tail. A white star, blaze, or stripe is found, but other white markings discouraged.
Character: Quiet, willing, dependable, friendly, agile.
Conformation: The Haflinger's short, slightly dished head, large dark eyes, neat ears, and fine nose give it an expressive, kindly appearance that reflects the Arabian blood in its past. It has a reasonable length of neck for a stocky pony, making it good to ride as well as for draft work. Its body is deep-girthed, muscular, and powerful.

I F you refer to this much-loved native equine as a pony, you would not be very popular with Icelanders. They always call the breed the Icelandic Horse, even though it rarely stands over 14hh.

This tough little horse has a long history and several unique features. The first horses arrived on this cold and remote island with the Norse settlers of the eighth and ninth centuries, surviving long and dangerous trips across the rough seas from Scandinavia and the Scottish islands.

The Icelandic breed is one of the purest in the world — no outside blood has been added for almost a thousand years.

Since that time, horses have had a special place in the lives of the island's people. Icelandics have been used for all kinds of work and are still one of the main forms of transportation in Iceland.

Today, owners also compete against each other in many sports, including racing, endurance rides, and even dressage. Many of the ponies live almost wild, despite the near-Arctic conditions. They are incredibly hardy. Besides being able to walk, trot, and gallop, Icelandics have two extra ancient gaits — a fast pacing movement called the *skeid*, and a running walk called the *tolt* — that help them cover rough ground with speed and agility.

Icelandic

DID YOU KNOW?

☙ THE Icelandic Horse eats herring that is caught by the island's fishermen.

☙ ICELANDIC Horses are famous for their homing instinct.

Place of origin: Iceland
Height: 12-14hh
Color: There are 15 official types and combinations with almost every color included.
Character: Hardy, friendly, energetic, surefooted, self-willed.
Conformation: The Icelandic has a large, heavy head for its size, with soft and intelligent eyes. The neck is short and well

FACT FILE

muscled, with a thick, bushy mane. The shoulders are upright; the body is deep and short in the back. The Icelandic has a low-set tail on sloping but very strong quarters. Its legs are short, but capable of carrying the weight of a man, at fast speeds, over a long distance.

Caspian

THE Caspian may be the most recently "discovered" breed, but it could well be the oldest of all. Scientists believe that it was from little horses, like the Caspian, that hot-blooded breeds, such as the Arabian, developed.

The Caspian has a remarkable story. Mysterious carvings from the ancient civilizations of Mesopotamia (around 3000 B.C.), Egypt, and later Persia, all showed tiny, perfectly proportioned horses. Yet, there were no records of these mini-Arabians for the past one thousand years, and it was presumed they were extinct.

Then, in 1965, a small herd was discovered on the shores of the Caspian Sea in northern Iran. The horses had the same features as the ones depicted in the ancient carvings. Many of these features were previously thought to have been unique to the Arabian horse. Because these ponies had never wandered from their home area and had not been crossbred, they provided fresh clues about how horses evolved. Small numbers of Caspians were exported to Britain, Australia, and America. They are excellent children's ponies and driving ponies.

DID YOU KNOW?

THE Caspian has a unique kind of red blood cell, a domed forehead unlike any other pony, and extra molars in the jaw. The shoulders and frontal vertebrae are built to make the Caspian narrower in the body than other breeds.

Fa

FALABELLA mares carry their foals an average of two months longer than other breeds — almost thirteen months. Newborn foals are just 16 inches (40 cm) tall at birth. They reach 90 percent of their height by the end of their first year.

Falabella

ALTHOUGH the Falabella is the world's smallest horse, it is not a pony. Falabellas are true miniature horses. They have all the features of a horse scaled down, rather than having pony proportions.

They are the most famous of many different miniature horses bred throughout history for people to keep as pets. Although these miniatures are now exported around the world, every one of them has originated from one place — the ranch of the Falabella family near Buenos Aires in Argentina.

There are many different stories concerning the Falabella's history. Señor Falabella tells of the appearance one day of a strange little horse at the river crossing by the mill of an early settler, named Newton, who was Falabella's grandfather.

The locals believed the horse suffered from "dwarf sickness." But, in fact, it was perfectly healthy and in proportion. So Newton decided to keep it to breed miniature horses for his daughter.

The stallion had the amazing ability to reduce the size of the offspring of any other mare he was crossed with. He became the foundation sire of the new mini-breed, which the family created using Shetlands and small examples of many larger breeds of different colors.

True Falabellas are extremely rare. They must come from the original Falabella stud. It is only the cross of two "tinies" that will produce another "tiny." It takes many generations for another cross to be shrunk down in size to a real miniature.

This has resulted in a lot of inbreeding, so the miniatures have lost their hardiness, despite having native pony blood.

Falabellas cannot be ridden, but they are appealing and affectionate pets that love company. Although they do not need a great deal of food, they are quite delicate and need careful management, just as if they were mini-Thoroughbreds.

FACT FILE

Place of origin: Argentina
Height: Not over 8.5hh
Color: All permissible
Character: Intelligent, friendly, and affectionate.
Conformation: Falabellas vary in looks according to what types have been used in their individual backgrounds. All have long, fine legs and narrow, short bodies, with two fewer ribs and vertebrae than other horses and ponies. Sometimes the legs are not particularly straight, which is a weakness breeders are trying to improve. Most Falabellas have a silky coat. The mane and tail are thick and luxurious.

DID YOU KNOW?

THE smallest horse on record was a miniature named Little Pumpkin that stood just 14 inches (35.5 cm) high and weighed 20 pounds (9 kg).

A Suffolk Punch mare and foal show the breed's stockiness and muscle power.

Working Horses

THESE are the giants of the horse world, the biggest and strongest of all the breeds. For centuries, "heavies" have played an important part in the economy as pulling power in agriculture and industry.

Workhorses are cold-bloods that are descended from these large, solid, cool-tempered heavy horses. Heavies developed in the cold, wet, forested regions of northern Europe.

Many breeds of heavy horses almost died out after they were replaced by tractors on the farms, and by trucks and railways for shipping and transportation.

These gentle giants are now being bred in greater numbers again. In some countries, horses are still used on farms or in forests where mechanization is difficult. Heavy horses are also used for draft work, such as pulling wagons. They make a spectacular sight at shows and demonstrations and in parades.

Shire

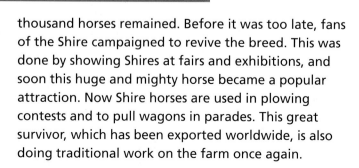

THE massive Shire is the world's tallest and heaviest horse. Its name comes from the Midland counties of England — the "shires" — where it was first bred. In the thirteenth century, King John imported one hundred huge horses from Holland to increase the size of the native English horses.

This was so the horses could carry heavily armored medieval knights, weighing up to 400 pounds (180 kg), into battle. In this way, the Great Horse of England came into being. Later, when guns replaced knights in armor, these Great Horses were used in the fields and, as roads improved, for heavy hauling.

The Great Horse was christened the *English Black* by English general and statesman Oliver Cromwell. The modern breed traces back to a foundation stallion called the Packington Blind Horse that was standing at stud in Leicestershire between 1755 and 1770. In 1884, the name *Shire* was adopted, and the breed became established.

Before the outbreak of World War II, Shires were widely used on farms. But, by the 1960s, barely two thousand horses remained. Before it was too late, fans of the Shire campaigned to revive the breed. This was done by showing Shires at fairs and exhibitions, and soon this huge and mighty horse became a popular attraction. Now Shire horses are used in plowing contests and to pull wagons in parades. This great survivor, which has been exported worldwide, is also doing traditional work on the farm once again.

FACT FILE

Place of origin: England (Midlands)

Height: Mares - from 16hh; stallions/geldings - at least 16.2hh; average height above 17hh

Color: Often black, also gray, brown, and bay — all with white feathering.

Character: Docile, gentle, sensible, very strong.

Conformation: The Shire has a medium-sized head with a broad forehead and kindly expression. It has a slightly convex profile, long ears, a long neck, and a very deep, wide shoulder for the harness collar to sit on. The barrel of a stallion is so huge that it can measure up to 8 feet (2.4 meters) around. Everything about the Shire's body is heavy, muscled, powerful, and compact, denoting its massive strength.

Clydesdale

THE Clydesdale is a relatively new working horse breed. It was specially created in Scotland, from the late eighteenth century onward, as a powerful draft horse that could be used for transportation, to work on the lowland farms, and to turn the machinery of the Industrial Revolution.

The first Clydesdales were bred from local, native mares crossed with bigger Flemish stallions. Later, many large black horses, the founders of the Shire breed, were imported from the English Midlands and used for breeding. This is partly why there are similarities between these two heavy breeds.

Soon the Clydesdale became famous for its strength and versatility and was exported as far as the United States, Canada, Japan, South Africa, and Australia. At home in Scotland, it is still used for forestry work and for pulling delivery vehicles, as well as for showing and competing in plowing contests. Some good showjumpers have Clydesdale blood in them.

FACT FILE

Place of origin: Scotland

Height: 16-18hh

Color: Bay, brown, black, or roan; with white face, stockings, and often a white underbelly.

Character: Very strong, steady, friendly, and cooperative.

Conformation: The Clydesdale always has a straight-profiled head and is never Roman-nosed like many heavy breeds. Its neck is quite long for a draft horse, and its shoulders are massively powerful. Together with its high-set withers, this equals great pulling power. Clydesdales have deep bodies but long legs, which have silky feathering around the lower limbs. Often the hocks turn inward ("cow hocks"). For a draft breed, it has very active, eye-catching movement.

Percheron

THIS handsome "heavy" from France is one of the oldest working horse breeds. Its name comes from the area of origin, La Perche, in the northwest region of the country.

You can see by its noble head and presence that there was a lot of Arabian and Asian blood used in the creation of this elegant and showy giant — just as there was with its cousin, the Boulonnais, France's other distinguished gray draft horse.

Horses left behind in France after the defeat of the Moors in A.D. 732 were probably crossed with strong Flemish workhorses to create the first Percherons.

More Arabian blood was added after the Crusades and, again, in the nineteenth century. During the Middle Ages, these proud and imposing heavyweights carried knights in armor. Later, they were in demand for agriculture and transportation, although they once again became war horses during World War I.

Today, numbers have decreased, but Percherons are still used on the farm and for hauling. They are exported worldwide for work and show.

Place of origin: France
Height: From 15.2-16.2hh on average, although can be bigger
Color: Mostly gray, sometimes black or roan.
Character: Strong, energetic, quiet, and good natured.
Conformation: The Percheron has a particularly fine and intelligent head with a wide forehead, straight face, bright eyes, and flared nostrils that show its Arabian ancestry. Its neck is quite long and arched, set into fairly sloping shoulders. This means its movement is not as choppy as many draft breeds. The body is short, deep, and strong, with large, powerful, rounded quarters. Its chunky legs have short cannon bones with little feathering. Percherons have especially good movement, which is long striding, free, and full of energy. Percherons are used as carriage horses and for riding.

FACT FILE

FACT FILE

Place of origin: Belgium, France

Height: 15-16.1hh

Color: Usually bay or roan, sometimes liver, chestnut, or dark gray.

Character: Exceptionally quiet, willing, very hardy, with good stamina.

Conformation: The head is small with a straight profile, prominent bright eyes, and alert, erect ears. It has a thick, upright neck, and a very deep, chunky body that oozes power and strength. Its short, stout legs are extremely strong and are heavily feathered.

Ardennes

THIS ancient heavy breed comes from Belgium and the north of France, where its forebears have lived for about two thousand years.

It is believed the Ardennes might be among the very earliest of the cold-blood breeds. Horses of this type were used by Caesar and other Roman emperors, who called them the "horses of Gaul." After Roman times, some Arabian blood was probably added to the local heavy horses to make them more elegant and active.

When more power was needed for agriculture and hauling, Belgian Heavy Horse (Brabant) crossbreeding added size and muscle. Napoleon was a great admirer of the Ardennes's toughness and strength, and he used the smaller, lighter horses for his armies.

Later, in World War I, the Ardennes pulled the artillery of the Dutch army. Today, Ardennes can still be seen working in the fields in northern France, Belgium, and Sweden, especially in hilly or forested areas.

DID YOU KNOW?

THE Ardennes is the smallest of the main heavy horse breeds.

THE Suffolk Punch is the oldest and purest of all England's heavy horse breeds. The name *Punch* comes from an old word for a horse meaning "short, fat fellow." This typifies the Suffolk Punch, famous for its chunky body.

Every Suffolk alive today can be traced back to a chestnut stallion, named *Crisp's Horse of Ufford*, foaled in 1768. Several centuries earlier, records tell of distinctive Suffolk farm horses, renowned for their strength. These may have been Flemish workhorses crossed with local trotters. During the nineteenth century, there were thousands of Suffolks working Fenland farms, but numbers dwindled after World War II when huge farm machinery moved onto the large, flat fields.

In 1966, only nine Suffolk foals were born, but a small group of breeders has been building the breed again. The Suffolk is famous for its pulling power and stamina. It has several features unique among the working breeds. It matures early and is very long-lived, often able to work well into its twenties. The Suffolk thrives on far less feed than other heavies and was traditionally able to work all day without a break.

Today, the Suffolk is still used for work on the farm, in the army, and in forestry.

Place of origin: Britain
Height: 16.2-17.2hh
Color: Chestnut, although seven different shades from light to liver are allowed. White permitted only on face.
Character: Kind, willing, sensible, hardy, and active.
Conformation: The Suffolk has a big, broad head and a short, thick neck, which is highlighted in the show ring with special decorations. The power comes from low-set muscular shoulders and a deep, round, compact body set on short, strong legs. Traditionally, breeders aimed for the legs to be set wide enough to give strength and stability, but set close enough not to walk in the plow's furrows. The Suffolk's active, balanced paces, relatively small feet, and sparse feathering are well suited to the heavy clay soils of the fields.

FACT FILE

Thoroughbred racehorses are the most valuable horses in the world.

No longer needed for transportation, many light draft breeds now excel in carriage driving trials.

Sports Horses

BARELY a century ago, almost every country in the western world had a large population of horses working at all kinds of jobs, from plowing to pulling carriages to carrying the cavalry to war.

Then, as machines took over almost all of these historical roles, the number of horses being bred plummeted. It seemed that many breeds — especially the heavy workhorses — were destined to die out. However, mechanization was not all bad news for the horse. It meant a life of less hardship for both horses and humans.

As people had more time for sports and leisure, they were able to see the horse as a friend and partner in fun and sports, rather than just as a working animal. Horse sports and pleasure riding became increasingly popular. This was accompanied by a growing demand for horses of the right shape and character for riding, and the athletic talent to be successful in competitions. Many old breeds were

Power and elegance are needed for dressage.

altered to make them better suited for riding sports. New breeds were created with specific features in order to excel at a particular activity. Sports horse breeds can all be classed either as hot-bloods or warm-bloods. The Arabian and Thoroughbred are the only true hot-blood breeds. They are the horse world's super-athletes — the star performers — especially in sports where speed or stamina is needed.

The other sports breeds are warm-bloods, created by carefully mixing hot-blood, cold-blood (heavy horse or native pony), and other warm-blood breeds. A breeder's aim is to combine the class, spirit, and agility of the hot-bloods with the reliable temperament and strength of the more solid breeds.

Event horses need to be fast, brave, and athletic. Most are Thoroughbreds.

FACT FILE

Place of origin: Middle East deserts

Height: Average of 15hh

Color: Gray, bay, chestnut, or black.

Character: Proud, highly strung, great stamina and presence, gentle, courageous.

Conformation: Arabians have a unique outline and look. The entire body is in perfect proportion. Their fine, tapering heads have large, flared nostrils, with large, low-placed eyes set very wide on the head. The Arabian profile is always dished. The ears are small and fine and often curve inward. The throat arches into the neck in a wide curve, and the neck is long, elegant, and curved. Arabians have an especially short, slightly dipped back and strong loins. They carry their tails high. This allows more air to flow around their quarters. This, together with a thin, silky coat, plus mane and tail hair, helps keep the body cool. The legs are fine and clean, with very hard, dense bone. The feet are suited to desert conditions. Arabians are known for their beautiful, floating stride.

MANY people would say that the Arabian is the most beautiful breed in the horse world. It is probably the oldest and purest, with records dating back as far as 3000 B.C.

The origins of this lovely and distinctive horse lie far back in time. Legend tells that the first person to capture and tame the wild ancestor of the Arabian was Noah's great-great-grandson, Baz.

The nomadic Bedouin tribespeople prized their desert horses beyond all other possessions. They carefully bred animals for beauty, stamina, and speed.

As the Muslim empire spread into Europe about a thousand years ago, so did its war horses. These horses were admired and valued throughout the Western world. The Arabian has been used to create and refine breeds, including the Thoroughbred, ever since. In fact, almost every breed and type has traces of Arabian blood.

Today, several different strains of Arabian have developed, though all are very carefully and strictly bred to keep the purity of the breed's features.

In eastern European countries, the Shagya Arabian is popular. It has slightly more substance than the pure desert Egyptian Arabian. Although Arabians are talented, all-around horses, the Thoroughbred and other specially bred performance breeds can usually beat them in most kinds of sport. However, the Arabian's famous stamina has made it a superstar at endurance riding. The exciting and glamorous world of Arabian racing has many fans. In the show ring, the breed is a breathtaking sight.

The

Arabian

DID YOU KNOW?

⊍ **EIGHTY-ONE** percent of the genes of all modern Thoroughbreds have been inherited from just thirty-one original horses.

⊍ **DURING** a race, a Thoroughbred's heart rate can increase from about 25 to 250 beats per minute!

No horse has ever been faster than the Thoroughbred, the equine world's "racing machine."

The speediest and most valuable of all breeds, a Thoroughbred changes hands for huge sums of money and is the basis for a worldwide, multi-million dollar racing business. Thoroughbreds are also champions in every other kind of horse sport.

The breed originated in the early 1700s in England, where kings and nobles were already using a mixture of eastern, Spanish, Italian, Irish, and Scottish-bred Galloway ponies as "running" horses.

King Charles II was a great racing fan and made Newmarket the headquarters of the sport. Soon everyone's attention turned to the interbreeding of the original racing stock with three imported Asian stallions — the Byerley Turk, the Godolphin Arabian, and the Darley Arabian. The pedigree of every modern Thoroughbred can be traced back through one of four lines founded by these horses.

By the end of the century, the breed was established. The General Stud Book began in 1793. It was closed not long afterward and, since then, no new stock has been added.

By then, the Thoroughbred could outrun any other horse. It was exported all over the world to improve other breeds. Within the breed itself, super-fast sprinters were bred to mature early for big-money races. Others matured later and were known for their stamina. Later, bigger and tougher strains were bred to be brave, tough racers over longer distances.

Thoro

When competitive riding became popular in the twentieth century, the Thoroughbred soon proved it was a great all-around athlete.

Breeders that wanted a calmer character and more substance crossed it with native and light draft breeds. Throughout the world, the Thoroughbred has helped produce versatile riding and sports horses. It has also added a touch of class to other breeds.

ughbred

Barb

THE hardy Barb was the horse of the nomadic desert tribespeople of Barbary — now the countries of Morocco, Algeria, and Libya.

These tough little horses have lived there since before the last Ice Age. The Barb has a lot in common with the Arabian. Even though the two breeds have been crossed a great deal over the centuries, they look quite different from each other and probably had separate origins.

Barbs taken to Spain during the Muslim occupation helped create the Spanish Horse and its relatives. The Barb's famous sprinting speed meant that many were imported to England and contributed to the Thoroughbred breed.

Today, there are few purebred Barbs left, but they can still be found in their desert homelands where they are as highly valued as ever.

DID YOU KNOW?

BARBS star in one of the most spectacular horse shows on earth — the Moroccan Fantasia, where thousands of tribesmen gather at dawn, mount their horses, and thunder in a flat-out gallop. They stand up in the stirrups, firing their rifles.

FACT FILE

Place of origin: North Africa
Height: 14-15.2hh
Color: Bay, brown, black, chestnut, or gray.
Character: Fiery, brave, with great stamina. Able to survive on little food.
Conformation: Unlike its Arabian cousin, the Barb has a heavy, narrow head with a concave or straight face. Its shoulders are rather flat and upright, and its body is deep, short, and strong. The Barb's quarters are rounded, but slope sharply, with a very low-set tail. Its legs are slender but tough, despite a tendency to poor conformation.

FACT FILE

Place of origin: Spain
Height: 15.1-15.3hh
Color: Usually gray, but can be bay, black, chestnut, or roan.
Character: Proud, active, willing, brave, athletic, spirited, but kind.
Conformation: The Andalusian's noble head has a broad forehead and slightly convex profile, with a rather haughty expression. The neck is muscular and arched, set into a long, sloping shoulder that helps its balanced and extravagant paces. Its body is deep and compact, with powerful quarters, and legs set well underneath. This, together with the flexion in its knee and hock joints, helps the Andalusian excel at the collected movements of high-stepping work. It has a long, full mane and tail, often very wavy.

FOR most of its history, the Andalusian has been known as the Spanish Horse. It is one of the most influential of all breeds.

Spanish Horses were created when tough, native Sorraia ponies were crossed with Barbs. The Barbs were brought to Spain by Muslims who occupied the country from the eighth to the fifteenth centuries.

During medieval times, the Spanish Horse became the war horse and the mount of royalty and aristocracy in Europe. With its noble presence and proud action, it became sought after for high-stepping work in the seventeenth and eighteenth centuries. It helped create the Lipizzaner breed as well as many other types of horses and ponies throughout Europe.

The *Conquistadores* took it to the New World, where it influenced most of the breeds of North and South America.

Today, the beautiful Andalusian is still loved and prized by the Spanish people.

It shows off its high-stepping work in the bullring and dressage arena. It is also a superb riding horse and showjumper — a favorite sight at fiestas.

Andalusian

Lusitano

FACT FILE

Place of origin: Portugal
Height: Mostly 15.1-15.3hh, although can be over 16hh
Color: Often gray or bay, but can be any solid color.
Character: Brave, full of life, eager to please, hard-working, gentle, agile.
Conformation: The Lusitano has a long, noble head that often has a slightly convex profile, but tapers to a fine, curved nose. It has large, kind, almond-shaped eyes and alert ears. Its neck is powerful, arched, and deep, but quite short and set upright. Power and strength come from a deep, compact body, muscled shoulders, and strong loins and quarters. It has plenty of silky hair in the mane and tail, and fine, lean, hard-boned legs with especially long cannon bones. The hind legs are set well under its body, which means it is naturally able to produce the collection, elevation, and impulsion that is needed in high-stepping work.

PROUD and spirited Lusitanos have been prized in their native Portugal and Spain for over five thousand years.

The breed is a cousin of the desert Barb and closely related to history's other classical horse, the Andalusian. Through the centuries, it has influenced many other continental and American breeds, although now it is quite rare. Only two thousand mares are left worldwide.

The same courage and intelligence that once made the Lusitano sought after for both war and high-stepping work are now put to use by Portuguese bullfighters.

The *rejoneadores* train their most talented horses to face and outwit (but not kill) the bull. The horses' skills are exhibited in parades before the fight. The breed also makes a strong farm, carriage, and riding horse. The Lusitano excels at dressage and showjumping.

Lipizzaner

LIPIZZANERS are world famous as the "dancing white horses" of the Spanish Riding School of Vienna, the renowned academy of classical riding that was founded in the seventeenth century.

This beautiful and distinguished breed was created from a shipment of thirty-three purebred Andalusian horses sent from Spain to the Imperial Austrian Stud at Lipizza (now in Croatia) in 1580. The proud, high-stepping horses were powerful, intelligent, and willing. These qualities made them perfect for the high-stepping work that was fashionable in Europe at the time.

The Spanish Riding School and its Lipizzaners have survived the political upheavals of central Europe. Today, they give demonstrations all around the world. Lipizzaners are still carefully bred from six lines that can be traced back to the early nineteenth century. After World War I, however, the breeding center was moved to Piber in southern Austria. Today, Lipizzaners perform at world-class dressage events, give exhibitions, do carriage driving, and work on farms in eastern Europe.

DID YOU KNOW?

DURING the Napoleonic Wars, three hundred horses were evacuated three times to escape the advancing French. In World War II, the Piber Stud was taken over by the Germans. Most of the mares were moved. A dramatic rescue in 1945 by a British army unit saved the breed from being scattered and lost.

Akhal-Teke

NO other horse breed looks quite like the Akhal-Teke of the central Asian deserts — with its amazing greyhound-like body and its coat that shines like polished metal.

This unique horse may have descended directly from one of the four basic subgroups of horses from which all breeds developed. It has a history going back four thousand years. Throughout the centuries, the nomadic tribesmen of the isolated region of Turkmenistan have prized their lean and leggy war horses, racing them, and keeping their breeding absolutely pure. Akhal-Tekes are famous for their speed, their incredible powers of endurance, and their ability to survive harsh extremes of temperature.

Traditionally, they were kept tethered and fed by hand — a diet of barley, alfalfa, sheep fat, eggs, and dough. Horses and herdsmen built a close relationship with each other.

Many horses still live a nomadic life in their homelands.

FACT FILE

Place of origin: Turkmenistan
Height: 14.2-15.2hh
Color: Bay, gray, black, chestnut, golden or silver dun, all with a distinctive sheen.
Character: Fast, spirited, brave, athletic, willful.
Conformation: The Akhal-Teke has a fine head with bold, prominent eyes. It has a straight face with wide-set, flared nostrils and large, alert ears. This is a breed that manages to be very athletic and tough, despite having many conformation faults. The neck is long, thin, and set upright. The back is very long and narrow, and the chest is shallow. It has weak loins, but the quarters are "lean and mean." The legs are long and fine and tend to be too close together. The breed is usually cow- and sickle-hocked. Even so, the movement is low and flowing. Manes and tails are sparse with fine hair.

DID YOU KNOW?

AKHAL-TEKES are officially the world's greatest endurance horses. In 1935, a group of them traveled over 2,500 miles (4,000 km) from Ashkabad to Moscow in eighty-four days. A quarter of the way was across arid desert. At one stage, the horses could not drink for three days.

FACT FILE

Place of origin: Germany (East Prussia)
Height: 16-16.2hh
Color: Any solid color, usually dark.
Character: Courageous, kind, athletic, with great stamina.
Conformation: The Trakehner has an especially fine head, full of quality and intelligence. It has wide-set, prominent eyes, upright ears, and a straight profile. Its neck is long and elegant. It has sloping shoulders, a deep chest, and a strong, level back. The quarters are rounded and powerful. The Trakehner's legs are shorter than a Thoroughbred's and have more bone. It has particularly good feet. The Trakehner is a very balanced horse with supple, flowing paces.

Trakehner

TRAKEHNERS are superstars at many modern horse sports. Almost every one of Germany's successful international teams has included an example of this historic warm-blood.

The famous Royal Trakehner Stud, which gave the breed its name, was founded in 1732 by King Frederick William I. However, horses based on hardy local breeds had been carefully bred in this area of Prussia for centuries before.

Soon horses from the Royal Stud were in demand throughout Europe as elegant coach horses. Then, as a succession of wars overtook Europe, these horses were in demand as a quality cavalry mount. So much Thoroughbred and Arabian blood was added that, by the twentieth century, the Trakehner was very much like the Thoroughbred in looks and temperament. By World War II, many thousands were being bred. The breed had a close call when the Stud was overtaken by the Russian army in 1945. A group of refugees managed to smuggle six hundred mares and foals, plus a few stallions, across the River Elbe on a 900-mile (1,450-km) journey to West Germany. Today's Trakehner was bred from these horses. Those that remained behind became the basis of Poland's Wielspolski breed.

Hanoverian

THE Hanoverian is another of Germany's talented warm-blood breeds, a star in the showjumping ring and dressage arena.

Hanoverian breeding has been very tightly controlled since it began. George II of Hanover and King of England founded the state stud in 1735 at Celle in Lower Saxony. Fourteen Holsteiner stallions and some local working mares were used.

At first, the idea was to produce strong all-around horses for farm work and transportation. But when Thoroughbred blood was added, the Hanoverian became a lighter breed, perfect for the cavalry and for pulling coaches.

By the middle of the twentieth century, sports horses were in demand. Attention turned to creating a breeding system that would produce some of the world's best equine athletes.

With the help of Trakehner and Arabian sires, the Hanoverian became a champion competition horse. Hanoverian breeding horses are selected only after passing strict tests for performance, soundness, and temperament. Today, Hanoverian breeding is a big business in Germany.

DID YOU KNOW?

ALL purebred Hanoverians are branded with a curved *H* mark on their quarters.

Holstein

THE impressive Holstein is believed to be the oldest of all the regional German breeds.

Today, like its relative the Hanoverian, the Holstein is a world-class sports and riding horse. But, when the first Holsteins were bred in the Middle Ages, they carried knights into battle. These early war horses were well known for their high-stepping movement.

Holsteins continued to be bred for war until the nineteenth century, but they became too heavy to be as useful as they once were. So breeders began to add Thoroughbred and Cleveland Bay blood to the original mix of native German, Spanish, Neapolitan, Yugoslavian, and eastern horses.

Soon, the Holstein's popularity increased again. It was in demand as a powerful and beautiful carriage horse. Holsteins excel at every kind of horse sport due to the recent adding of more and more Thoroughbred blood.

FACT FILE

Place of origin: Germany (Schleswig-Holstein)

Height: 16-17hh

Conformation: The Holstein has a medium-sized, quality head, with alert eyes and ears. The neck is long and slightly arched. The shoulder is sloping and deep. The body is well shaped with rounded, powerful quarters, and strong, clean, well-formed legs. This is a tall, handsome riding horse with very balanced, flowing paces.

DID YOU KNOW?

THE Holstein almost died out after World War II, but numbers have increased since the 1960s. At the 1984 Olympics, 70 percent of the German equestrian team members rode horses of Holstein breeding.

World champion dressage star Marzog, ridden by Anne-Grethe Jensen of Denmark, is a Danish warm-blood.

DID YOU KNOW?

Many breeds of French horses have been merged to create the Selle Francais. There are different types for racing, general riding, and competition. Pierre Durand's Olympic showjumping champion, Jappeloup, was a Selle Francais with Thoroughbred and Trotter breeding.

Europe's Warm-bloods

DURING the twentieth century, most European countries developed their own national warm-blood horses. The horses were often based on local breeds previously used for pulling carriages or as cavalry mounts.

Breeders soon realized that the strength and steady character of these light draft types were valued by competition riders. The riders wanted powerful horses with flowing, balanced paces and obedient natures for the sports of dressage and showjumping. Upgraded by using Thoroughbreds and other hot-bloods for added spirit and agility, these new continental warm-bloods have become superb equine performers.

Britain's Tanya Larrigan with her Olympic dressage horse Salute, a Swedish warm-blood.

Nick Skelton competing on one of his most successful horses, the Dutch-bred Apollo.

Cleveland Bay

BIG bay horses have been bred and used as pack animals since the Middle Ages — and maybe even earlier — in the northeast of Yorkshire in northern England. They used to be called Chapman's Horses because they traditionally carried merchandise of the door-to-door salesmen of the day, known as chapmen.

Originally, the Romans probably brought horses to this area. Over the centuries, trade with North Africa introduced Spanish and Barb horses. The mixture resulted in a strong-backed, clean-legged horse that could carry wool and iron ore from the hills to the ports.

Clevelands were also used on the land, ridden by local farmers and hunters. In the heyday of carriage transportation, many Clevelands were crossed with Thoroughbreds to create a fast, classy type with great stamina. This new crossbreed was called the Yorkshire Coach Horse, and it became the most famous carriage horse in the world.

Sadly, things changed with the arrival of the train, the car, and the tractor. Just as the breed was about to die out, people realized what talented sports horses Cleveland Bays and their crossbreeds could be. Today, they can be seen showjumping, in dressage, and in carriage-driving trials. They are also superb hunters and police horses.

FACT FILE

Place of origin: Britain (North Yorkshire)

Height: 16-16.2hh

Color: Bay with black points. A little gray hair allowed in the mane and tail. No white allowed, except a small star.

Character: Docile, easy to train, versatile, hardy.

Conformation: The Cleveland has a bold head, sometimes with a convex profile, which is similar to the Spanish Andalusian horses that appear in its ancestry. It has a lean but powerful neck and shoulder, a very deep girth, and strong, round quarters. A Cleveland's legs are relatively short but have plenty of bone. The legs have no feather, allowing the legs to be lifted clear of the heavy clay soil while working on the farm or hunting in homeland areas.

DID YOU KNOW?

AN Irish farm horse's winter diet was made of chaff, boiled turnips, and bran or meal left over from the cows' dinner. No wonder the Irish Draft is still an easy-keeper!

Irish Draft

THE Irish pride themselves on producing hunting, jumping, and cross-country horses that are in demand throughout the world.

Most of these are produced using Thoroughbreds crossed with the Irish Draft.

Far from being the heavy that its name implies, the Irish Draft is Ireland's all-arounder — a big, strong, handsome horse that is still athletic and light on its feet.

Its history goes back to the small Irish farm where it was expected to be a plow horse, pull the cart to market and church, and go on the hunt several times a week. Ireland's original stock came from a mixture of French and Flemish farm horses that were improved by adding Andalusian blood.

The country's rich pastures helped the breed grow strong and sound. The Irish love of hunting made the horses agile and clever.

The breed was almost lost several times during various periods of poverty and famine in Ireland.

However, it has now been recognized for its fine qualities and versatility. It is highly valued as breeding stock that gives substance and common sense to lighter breeds. This creates winning performance horses in every kind of international horse sport.

Place of origin: Holland
Height: 14.3-15.3hh
Color: Black, with no more white than a small star
Character: Great presence, kind, lively, sensible.
Conformation: The Friesian has a long, handsome head with gentle, expressive eyes. Its neck is crested and proudly held, with the mane long and full like the tail. The body is built for strength, deep and compact with rounded quarters. Its limbs are short and strong, with feathering up to the knees or hocks. It has a spirited, high-stepping trot.

THE showy, stocky Friesian can claim to be one of Europe's oldest horses, an ancestor of the primitive "Forest Horse" that was the forerunner of the heavies.

It is bred in the north of the Netherlands in Friesland, an area of rich grassland. It was the strong, but active, Friesian that the Romans used as their workhorse. Friesians later carried the medieval knights to the Crusades. Over the centuries, the breed's appearance was improved by adding eastern and Spanish blood. It developed into a very handsome work and light draft horse, with a spectacular trot.

Friesians were also used to improve breeds from many neighboring countries. Those taken to Britain by the Romans helped create the Fell and Dales ponies, as well as the Shire horse. The Shire is commonly black, showing its Friesian ancestry.

Friesians have been used for many jobs in the past, especially in funeral processions. Today, they star in the circus ring, in driving competitions, and as beautiful and eye-catching carriage horses.

Friesian

Hackney

DURING the golden era of carriage driving in Victorian times, it was the height of fashion to be seen in your own private carriage pulled by a Hackney horse.

Whether you were driving yourself or being driven by a coachman, this elegant, high-stepping breed with its fast, spectacular trot was the Porsche of harness horses.

It is thought that the word *hackney* comes from *haquenee*, an early French word meaning "nag for hire." The breed is based on the tough and speedy trotting horses traditionally used by farmers in Lincolnshire, East Anglia, and east Yorkshire to drive and ride to the market. Some of these early trotters were famous for amazing feats of endurance. Farmers used to place bets on whose horse was the fastest or had the greatest stamina.

Breeding became organized, and the Hackney was soon in demand as a carriage horse for private and trade vehicles. A pony type was also created with the same brilliant action. In the twentieth century, Hackneys were no longer needed as workers. But they are so loved for their flashy style that they have remained popular in the show ring. They turn heads in the private driving and *concours d'elegance* class, becoming combined driving champions. They have also improved other breeds around the world and have created elegant saddlehorses.

Place of origin: Britain
Height: Horses — over 14hh-15.3hh; ponies — under 14hh
Color: Usually brown, bay, black, or chestnut.
Character: Full of personality, confident, loves to show off, quick, athletic, brave, and proud.
Conformation: The Hackney has a small head with a convex profile, and large ears and eyes. The head is always carried high and with spirit. Its neck is long and set almost vertically from very low withers and strong shoulders. Its compact body is silky coated, and the tail is carried high. Though the Hackney does not have long legs, the hocks are set low. It stands proudly with its hind legs out behind.

FACT FILE

HARNESS racing is a popular sport throughout the world. In many European and Scandinavian countries, it has more fans than any other form of racing.

Throughout history, many countries have tried to produce speedy trotting and pacing horses to race in harness, pulling light, two-wheeled "sulkies." Among the best were England's Norfolk Roadster and Russia's Orlov Trotter, but the American Standardbred is the fastest of all. This breed was made possible by the creation of the Thoroughbred. It was founded from an early English Thoroughbred, named *Messenger*, brought to the United States in 1788.

Although breeding was not very organized at first, with many different trotting-type mares used, almost every Standardbred can be traced back to one of four of Messenger's sons — in particular, a descendant named *Hambletonian 10*. As trotting races became more popular, breeding became more organized. In 1879, one-mile speed "standards" were set — and so the breed got its name. Known for their incredible short bursts of speed, Standardbreds are also champion racehorses. They are exported worldwide. Separate races are held for trotters and for pacers. Pacers move the pair of legs on the same side of the body at the same time.

FACT FILE

Place of origin: United States
Height: 14-16hh, average 15.2hh
Color: Bay, brown, black, and chestnut.
Character: Fast, willing, competitive, brave.
Conformation: The Standardbred is like a slightly stockier, more robust Thoroughbred. It doesn't have the same quality look, but it has very long, strong shoulders. The withers are often lower than the powerful, rounded quarters, which have a high croup (rump) — this is what gives the breed its amazing acceleration and thrusting paces. The legs, which are shorter than a Thoroughbred's, must be very hard, correct, and straight in their stride to avoid injury at high speeds.

Standardbred

America's Gaited Breeds

THE UNITED STATES boasts three spectacularly showy breeds that have extra gaits, or paces, besides the normal walk, trot, and canter. The **American Saddlebred, Tennessee Walking Horse,** and **Missouri Fox Trotter** all originated in the southern states during the nineteenth century.

They were practical performers that could give an easy and comfortable ride, all day long, inspecting the plantations, have the speed to race, and still turn heads under saddle or in harness. The breeds are closely related. They all have their roots in naturally gaited ambling and pacing horses of Spanish and Galloway stock brought to America by the first British settlers. These were developed into the Narragansett Pacer of Rhode Island and Virginia. During the 1700s and 1800s, Thoroughbred blood helped create the "American Horses" that were the basis of the gaited breeds.

The **American Saddlebred**, originally from Kentucky, performs in the show ring with three or five gaits. The three-gait horse shows a highly collected, animated walk, trot, and canter. The five-gaited horse is trained to also produce a four-beat prancing movement called the "slow gait," and a unique high-flying, smooth-flowing "rack."

The **Tennessee Walking Horse** has three natural, unique gaits — the flat-foot walk, the running walk, and the rocking-chair canter. All are fast, gliding movements that make an impressive sight and give a very comfortable ride. Both of these breeds have a natural talent to perform quite differently from any other horses. Showing enthusiasts use very different training and presentation techniques from the traditional English style in order to accentuate presence and stride. Outside the

DID YOU KNOW?

THE American Saddlebred was the flashy mount favored by generals during the American Civil War. TV stars of the '50s — Champion the Wonder Horse, Flicka, and Mr. Ed — were Saddlebreds.

The Saddlebred (above) *is America's number one show horse.*
Inset: *The Tennessee Walking Horse, like all the gaited breeds, has extremely comfortable, rolling paces.*

A Tennessee Walking Horse stallion (opposite).

show ring, both breeds make versatile pleasure, trail, and competition horses. They are also stars of the circus and screen.

The **Missouri Fox Trotter** is a more compact, plainer-looking horse than its elegant cousins. The breed was developed to be hardy and surefooted in the mountains of Missouri. It has a particularly unusual, low, floating gait. The horse walks in front and, at the same time, trots behind with a peculiar sliding action of the hind feet. Fox Trotters are famous for keeping up this active and stylish "Fox Trot" over long distances.

Quarter Horse

KNOWN as "America's Horse," the Quarter Horse is the oldest breed in the United States. With almost three million registered, it can also claim to be the most popular breed in the world and is extremely versatile. With breathtaking sprinting ability, a Quarter Horse can go from a standing start to 40 miles (65 km) per hour in one stride, stop just as quickly, spin on a dime, and twist and turn in perfect balance. It can live on the barest pasture and work hard all day long.

The breed's history begins with the first English settlers, who crossed imported horses of native Asian blood with the hardy, quick-thinking Indian ponies of Spanish and Barb ancestry that were already in America.

Later, Thoroughbred blood was introduced. The result was a compact, muscled horse, with massively powerful quarters, that could work the farms and plantations by day and, on weekends, satisfy the colonists' love of racing using explosive sprinting ability.

Horses were pitted against each other in nail-biting match races down streets or meadows for a quarter of a mile — which is how the breed got its name. It became unbeatable at this distance.

Later, as pioneers moved West, the Quarter Horse was adopted as the "cowboy's horse." Its agility, toughness, sense of balance, and natural "cow-savvy" is legendary.

Today, Quarter Horse racing is a multi-million dollar business in the United States. These power-packed horses can be seen at the racetrack, at rodeos, at Western riding shows, on the trails, and participating in many horse sports throughout the world.

DID YOU KNOW?

A Quarter Horse can cover a distance of 1/4 mile (0.5 km) in 21 seconds. The fastest racehorses have been clocked at nearly 55 miles (85 km) per hour!

THE world's richest horse race is the All-American Futurity for three-year-old Quarter Horses.

T HIS talented Morgan breed has style with a capital *S*. Its proud looks and spirit, like the horses of the Old Master paintings, have made it America's own "classical horse."

No one knows the original breeding of the Morgan, although Arabian, Thoroughbred, Friesian, and Welsh Cob blood may have played a part. Every Morgan is descended from a single dark bay stallion.

During the 1790s, this horse was given to a Vermont music teacher named Justin Morgan as part payment of a debt. This legendary little horse, named after its owner, stood only 14hh. But it soon gained a reputation far and wide for its ability to outrace, outpull, outdistance, and outshine all other horses. It also thrived on the poorest pasture.

In addition, whatever the mare, its offspring matured early into exact copies of itself — and so the breed was born. Morgans were soon being bred as classy all-arounders, that could work on the plantation, pull a light buggy, or step out stylishly under saddle.

A unique style of riding grew up with the breed, known as "saddle seat" or "Park seat," which helped show off the horse's extravagant, floating stride. Special methods of management were developed to enhance the breed's beauty and presence, including trimming the feet and mane, and using a unique saddle and bridle. Known for its intelligence, good manners, and friendliness, the breed has many fans worldwide.

It is an ideal family horse, a competitor in many sports, and has contributed to several other American breeds.

DID YOU KNOW?

AFTER passing tough performance tests, the Morgan was chosen as the official mount of the U.S. Army. Today, Morgans are still used by many mounted police squads.

Morgan

FACT FILE

Place of origin: U.S.A. (New England)
Height: Average 14.2 - 15.3hh
Color: Bay, brown, black or chestnut; only occasionally palomino, dun, or gray.
Character: Brave, docile, intelligent, tough, friendly, a great presence.
Conformation: The Morgan has a fine, tapering head with a straight or slightly dished profile, large nostrils, bold eyes, and small, erect, wide-set ears. Its neck is crested with a clean-cut throat-lash. Its strong shoulders slope well, and its body is short, broad, and muscled with a deep, round barrel and wide chest. The legs are slender but strong, with short cannons. Morgans have long, silky manes and tails.

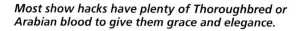

Most show hacks have plenty of Thoroughbred or Arabian blood to give them grace and elegance.

Horse and

Crossbreeds with a purpose

AS well as the different breeds of horses and ponies, there are also various different "types." Instead of belonging to a breed that has a Stud Book or pedigree, a "type" is produced by crossing breeds to get a horse or pony that is especially well suited for a particular purpose. In the United Kingdom, some are produced for the show ring and must adhere to certain specifications. The best-known types include the Hunter, the Hack, the Cob, the Riding Pony, and the Polo Pony.

HUNTER

ANY horse or pony that follows hounds could be called a hunter. Types vary depending on the local countryside. However, the typical hunter is a Thoroughbred crossed with a heavier breed, such as the Irish Draft or Cleveland Bay, or with one of the bigger British native ponies. Good hunters are well put together; they are strong and brave and have lots of stamina and

A typical hunter type stallion.

good manners. They must be a very comfortable ride with easy, balanced paces and an especially good gallop and jump. Most are 16-16.2hh.

HACK

HACKS are classy Thoroughbred or Anglo-Arabian riding horses with perfect paces, looks, and manners. This type developed from the days when grooms would ride hunters to a meet, and the owner would follow behind on his showy hack.

Hacks did not have to hunt all day, so they were more lightly built than a hunter. The "park hack" was used by fashionable ladies and gentlemen to show off when riding in the park. It was expected to behave impeccably and to have a floating, eye-catching stride.

COB

THESE stocky little horses, with round bodies and short legs, have been popular since the Middle Ages as the mounts of farmers and squires. The name *cob* was first used in the 1700s. Only the Welsh Cob is a proper breed in its own right. Most cobs are bred from hunter stock with some pony or draft horse added, and maybe a touch of Thoroughbred.

Cobs are usually kind, sensible, and safe rides, but they are energetic and often have lots of character. They are ideal as hunters over rough country, for heavy riders, novice riders, or as a family horse.

Pony Types

A riding pony is perfect for a child. It has beautiful manners, movement, and looks.

A cob is a stout, stocky little horse with good manners and a wonderful personality.

RIDING PONY

ALTHOUGH any pony used for riding could be called a riding pony, many countries have created an ideal child's pony with this name just for the show ring. Riding ponies often look like mini-Thoroughbreds, although most are a mix of Thoroughbred, Arabian, and native breeds.

Breeders aim to produce the presence and style of the hot-bloods combined with pony good sense and soundness.

A winning pony must have substance but be all class and quality, with faultless conformation, straight and true paces, and first-class temperament and manners. It is a perfect pony for a child.

POLO PONY

DESPITE usually being over 14.2hh, polo ponies are always called ponies. When the ancient game of polo was first played in northern India, small local breeds were used. But, today, most polo ponies are crosses between small Thoroughbreds and other breeds, such as the Criollo, the Argentinian gaucho's cow pony. Argentina produces the fastest, toughest,

and cleverest polo ponies in the world, although the ponies are bred wherever the game is popular, including the United States and Britain.

Polo ponies look like wiry little Thoroughbreds. They are brave, agile, sound, speedy, and fit. The best ones are very bright and have an uncanny instinct for the game.

Polo ponies must be brave and agile.

Color Breeds

FOUR coat colors are recognized as different breeds in the United States, although, in the rest of the world, they are considered to be "types" rather than true breeds.

PALOMINO

AROUND the world, many breeds and types include the beautiful golden palomino coloring, with its pale mane and tail. But this color is unknown in pure Arabians or Thoroughbreds.

The eye-catching golden color has been popular throughout history. Today, palominos are especially in demand for showing and Western riding. The palomino is not a real breed because it does not breed true to type, and there is no guarantee that the offspring of two palominos will be a palomino itself. However, registered American palominos must be over 14hh and have one parent of either Quarter Horse, Arabian, or Thoroughbred blood, so most are either quality show horses or stocky cow-pony types. Most countries have palomino societies that register horses of suitable color and type.

APPALOOSA

SPOTTED horses and ponies have been around since the time of the prehistoric cave dwellers. They have been highly prized over the centuries throughout Europe and Asia. Spanish stock taken to the New World brought the coloring to America. Soon the Nez Percé Indians, whose lands bordered the Palouse River in Oregon, were breeding tough, reliable, and agile spotted horses for war and hunting. These horses were almost wiped out along with the Indians in the 1870s, but enthusiasts revived the "breed." Today, America's register of them is one of the largest in the world.

Most Appaloosas are 14.2-15.2hh. In the United States, they are usually chunky, cow-pony types with fine legs and a sparse mane and tail. European Appaloosas are often taller with less of a Quarter Horse shape. Just like in the United States, the only crosses permitted for registration are with Arabians, Quarter Horses, or Thoroughbreds. Britain has a small type called the British Spotted Pony.

At one time, Palominos were called Isabellas *after the Queen of Spain, who loved their golden color.*

⚘ THERE are eight basic Appaloosa coat patterns: *Snowflake* (dark with white spots all over), *Leopard* (white with dark spots all over), *Frosted hip* (dark with white spots or speckles over quarters), *Marble* (mottled roan

Spotted horses have appeared in various breeds over the centuries. This is a British Spotted Pony.

A leopard spotted Appaloosa.

or bay with darker patches), *White blanket* (dark forehand, white over quarters without spots), *Spotted blanket* (dark forehand, white over quarters with spots), *Near leopard* (leopard spotted body but different color head and legs), and *Few-spot leopard* (white with a few roan patches or spots).

The skin is mottled, the eye is always encircled by white, and the hooves are often striped. No two Appaloosas have exactly the same markings.

True Albinos (right) have no pigment or coloring.

ALBINO

O CCASIONALLY, albinos crop up in many breeds. Because the "coloring" always breeds true, the albino is being established as a breed in the United States. It is based on the offspring of a stallion called Old King, foaled in 1906.

True albinos have no pigment, so they all have very sensitive pink skin and blue eyes.

Color breeds

The eye-catching Overo type of Pinto has white splashes on a dark base coat. The head is usually white. The other, more common, coloring type is the Tobiano, featuring regular solid patterns of dark on a white horse.

PINTO

THE Pinto, or Paint Horse, is a descendant of Spanish horses brought to America by the *Conquistadores*.

American Indians of earlier times loved the broken coloring that provided good camouflage. Later, the Pinto became a popular color with the cowboys of the Wild West. Pintos can be found worldwide, and many countries have registers for them. The biggest and most famous is the Pinto Horse Association of America.

There is great variety in its size and type, but the American Pinto is often a small stock horse with a compact body, fine legs, and sensible character.

ass — an animal species found wild in Asia. It is gray in color and is known for its determination and strength.

barrel — the part of a horse or pony's body around the ribs.

breed (horse/pony) — a group of horses or ponies that has been carefully reproduced for particular features over many years.

cold-blood — a heavy breed of horse used for work on farms, for transportation, and in industry.

conformation — the overall shape and appearance of a horse or pony.

cow-hocks — hocks, or regions in the hind limbs, that turn in like a cow's.

crossbreeding (horses/ponies) — when a horse/pony of one breed is mated with a horse/pony of another.

dished face — when the front of the head dips in (concave).

dock — the solid part of a tail.

domesticate — tame.

dorsal stripe — a dark line running down the neck and backbone.

draft horse — a heavy horse used for pulling carts and machinery. Light draft breeds are used in harness for pulling carriages.

dressage — the execution by a horse or pony of precision movements in response to signals from a rider.

dun — a variable color but usually a nearly neutral brownish dark gray.

feather — long hair on the lower legs, often found on cold-blood breeds.

foal — any young horse or pony up to the age of one year.

forehand — the front half of a horse or pony, in front of the saddle.

gait — the way a horse or pony moves. Most horses or ponies have four gaits — walk, trot, canter, and gallop. Some breeds have special, additional gaits.

hand — a 4-inch (10.2-cm) unit of measurement to describe the height of a horse or pony. Measurement is taken from the ground to the highest point of the shoulder (the withers).

horse — a large hoofed animal of the Equidae family that is over 14.2 hands high.

hot-blood — a horse purebreed of very fine quality, like the Arabian or Thoroughbred.

mare — an adult female horse.

pacer — a horse that trots using the pair of legs on the same side moving together.

pedigree — a registry recording ancestral line. Many species have registered pedigrees.

pony — a large hoofed animal of the Equidae family that is under 14.2 hands high.

Roman nose — a rounded (convex) face, common in draft breeds.

sickle hocks — when viewed from the side, sickle hocks bend in under the body.

sloping shoulders — a feature where the line of the shoulders runs at about 45 degrees from the withers to the front of the chest. This gives a free-moving stride. Straight shoulders have a more upright line; they are strong but give a choppy stride.

solid color — a color that has no patches.

stallion — an adult male horse that can breed.

stride — the way a horse or pony moves.

type — a group of horses or ponies that does not belong to a breed. The horses and ponies in the group look similar and are bred for a particular purpose.

warm-blood — a horse breed created by crossing breeds — usually a mix of hot-blood and cold-blood.

zebra marks — stripes on the legs and sometimes on the neck and quarters of a horse or pony that resemble a zebra's.

The New Forest pony has a free, low, long-striding action suited to the Forest environment.

Books

The Encyclopedia of the Horse. Elwyn Hartley Edwards (Dorling Kindersley)

Horses. Animal Families (series). Hans D. Dossenbach (Gareth Stevens)

Horses of the World. Daphne Machin Goodall (Macmillan)

Magnificent Horses of the World (series). T. Mícek & H.J. Schrenk (Gareth Stevens)

The Nature of Horses. Stephen Budiansky (The Free Press)

The Random House Book of Horses and Horsemanship. Paula Rodenas (Random House)

The Saddle Club (series). Bonnie Bryant (Gareth Stevens)

Stable Girl. Patricia H. Easton (Harcourt)

Videos

The Art of Riding. (Visual Education Productions)

Ballad of the Irish Horse. (Image Entertainment)

Basic Horsemanship from the Ground Up. (Visual Education Productions)

A Breakthrough for Breaking In. (Visual Education Productions)

Dressage: The Horse in Sport. (Discovery Trail)

The Horse. (Barr Media)

The Horse Family. (International Film Bureau)

Horsemanship: The Fundamentals. (Videoactive)

Web Sites

www.cowgirls.com/dream/jan/rodeo.htm

www.ansi.okstate.edu/breeds/horses/

www.imh.org/

www.blm.gov/whb/

www.yahoo.com/Business/Corporations/ Animals/Horses

Index